DOES GOD REALLY CARE ABOUT POLITICS?

God and Government

Rochelle Conner

ISBN No. 9781642370287
Religion/Politics

Scriptural References:
Authorized King James Version (KJV)

Printed in the United States of America 2006

Published by
Per-Fect Words Publishing Company
www.per-fectwords.com

Foreword

After reading this book, my first thought as a leader in the body of Christ, was that I have not done my part in the political realm of the Kingdom. I now accept the fact that, if I am not part of the solution then, I am certainly part of the problem. Through this woman of integrity, I have been challenged to leave the four walls of the church and proactively address the needs of God's people through a new enlightenment of the political process. For years I have voted on the Democratic ticket because my father did and his father before him. Through this book I discovered that, "my stand on societal issues is greater than my familiar party of choice."

Rochelle has inspired me, as a Bishop in the Lord's church, to motivate the Pastors that I oversee, and their congregations, to educate themselves concerning the church's role in the political arena. It is imperative that we make informed choices concerning the governmental officials that are placed in authority over us. The Bible states, "when the righteous are in authority the people rejoice; when the wicked bear rule, the people mourn.

My prayer is that this book will open the eyes of every believer and cause them to begin to exercise, in greater numbers, our God given authority to make a difference and change the atmosphere.

– Bishop Anthony L. Willis, Senior Pastor
Lily of the Valley Christian Center
Oakland, CA

Acknowledgments

I want to thank the historians and researchers at Justice at the Gate and Wallbuilders who supplied much of the historical data for this book. It is with humble gratitude that I acknowledge their commitment and dedication to bring to light hidden truths that many have worked to hide. Thank you for revealing the intricate details many history writers have left hidden from view. It was a pleasure and an honor to use many references of your work here. May God continue to give you the courage and fortitude to make known truths that set us free.

Author's Comments

To the readers of this book, some things may come as a surprise, some things may confirm your own beliefs, some things may challenge your traditions, some things may even stir you to ire. Considering the times in which we live, I feel the urgent need to cry aloud and spare not. The night is far spent and the day is at hand, we must cast off the works of apathy, indifference, fatalism, irresponsibility, and take up arms. We are at war. Choose ye this day whom ye will serve. I encourage you to read, read, read and read some more, question, think, ponder, look, listen, engage in healthy debate and then....occupy until He returns.

Table of Contents

Chapter 1

DOES GOD REALLY CARE ABOUT POLITICS?

---●---

CIVIL GOVERNMENT IS ORDAINED BY GOD

All powers of civil authority are ordained by God.

> Let every soul be subject unto the higher powers,
> For there is no power but of God: the powers
> that be are ordained of God. Whosoever therefore
> resisteth the power, resisteth the ordinance of
> God: and they that resist shall receive to
> themselves damnation. For rulers are not a terror
> to good works, but to the evil. Wilt thou then
> not be afraid of the power? Do that which is good
> and thou shalt have praise of the same. For he is
> the minister of God to thee for good. But if thou
> do that which is evil, be afraid; for he beareth not
> the sword in vain; for he is the minister of God; a
> revenger to execute wrath upon him that doeth
> evil. Wherefore ye must needs be subject, not
> only for wrath, but also for conscience sake. For
> this cause pay ye tribute also: for they are God's
> ministers, attending continually upon this very
> thing. Render therefore to all their dues; tribute
> to whom tribute is due; custom to whom custom;
> fear to whom fear; honour to whom honour.
> Romans 13:1-7

God has ordained law and order in society. Laws of order are imperative for a well-functioning society. We have laws to protect us from unscrupulous business transactions (Uniform Commercial Code); laws to protect us from tyranny (US Constitution); laws enacted by agencies to protect us as we travel

(National Safety and Transportation Board; Department of Transportation); there are endless laws, ordinances, and statutes that are intended to protect us. How did these laws come into effect? Some laws (legislation) are enacted by elected officials. Policies and regulations can be enacted by elected officers or administrative agencies, i.e. city councils, school boards, parks and recreation committees, etc.

In reviewing biblical history, it is evident that God condoned the institution of a political process. In the Book of Exodus chapter 18, the Bible records:

> And it came to pass on the morrow, that Moses sat down to *judge* the people; and the people stood by Moses from the morning unto the evening. And when Moses' father in law saw all that he did to the people, he said, What is this thing that thou doest to the people? Why sittest thou thyself alone and all the people stand by thee from morning unto even? And Moses said unto his father in law, Because the people come unto me to enquire of God: *When they have a matter, they come unto me; and I judge between one and another, and I do make them know the statutes of God and his laws.* And Moses' father in law said unto him, The thing that thou doest is not good. Thou wilt surely ware away, both thou, and this people that is with thee; for this thing is too heavy for thee; thou art not able to perform it thyself alone. Hearken now unto my voice, and I will give thee counsel, and God shall be with thee: Because that thou mayest bring the causes unto God; and thou shall teach them ordinances and

laws, and shall shew them the way wherein they must walk, and the work that they must do. *Moreover thou shall provide out of all the people able men, such as fear God, men of truth, hating coveteousness; and place such over them, to be rulers of thousands, and rulers of hundreds, rulers of fifties, and rulers of tens: and let them judge the people at all seasons and it shall be that every great matter they shall bring unto thee, but every small matter they shall judge:* so shall it be easier for thyself, and they shall bear the burden with thee. If thou shalt do this thing, and God command thee so, then thou shalt be able to endure, and all this people shall also go to their place in peace. So Moses hearkened to the voice of his father in law, and did all that he had said. *And Moses chose able men out of all Israel and made them heads over the people, rulers of thousands, rulers of hundreds, rulers of fifties, and rulers of tens. And they judged the people at all seasons; the hard causes they brought unto Moses, but every small matter they judge themselves.*

Wow, here is the judicial branch of civil government in action. Moses is the head judge ordained by God tasked to judge matters between the people and to make known to them God's laws and statutes. But, because there were so many people with issues to be resolved and the time required to adjudicate each matter, Jethro, Moses's father-in-law offers wise counsel that results in the establishment of a judicial system. A judicial flow chart may help to visualize the analogy:

MOSES	SUPEREME COURT	NATION
Rulers of Thousands	Appellate Court	State
Rulers of Hundreds	Superior Court	Counties
Rulers of Fifties	Municipal/District Court	Cities
Rulers of Tens	Arbitration/Mediation	Neighborhood/ Community

The process flows upward from the people to local judges, to appellate judges, to supreme court justices.

In Deuteronomy 16:18 Moses authorizes the people to select judges and officers, a model of representative government. "Judges and officers shalt thou make thee in all thy gates, which the Lord thy God giveth thee, throughout thy tribes: and they shall judge the people with just judgment." Israel's civil government was administered by judges until King Saul was selected and anointed by God to govern the nation.

———————⬤———————

CIVIL GOVERNMENT IN THE NEW TESTAMENT

In the New Testament we see the [s] "election" process in action:

> And in those days, when the number of disciples was multiplied, there arose a murmuring of the Grecians against the Hebrews because their widows were neglected in the daily ministration. Then the twelve called the multitude of the disciples unto them, and said, it is not reason that we should leave the word of God

and serve tables. Wherefore, brethren, look ye out among you seven men of honest report, full of the Holy Ghost and wisdom, whom we may appoint over this business. But we will give ourselves continually to prayer, and to the ministry of the word. And the saying pleased the whole multitude and they chose Stephen, a man full of faith and of the Holy Ghost, and Philip and Prochorus, and Nicanor, and Timon, and Parmenas, and Nicholas, a proselyte of Antioch.

Acts 6:1-5

The *multitude chooses men* to administer social services: *representatives are elected by the people.* It is conceivable that names of *nominees/candidates* would be submitted for consideration; credentials/qualifications would be scrutinized; and a *vote* taken *to* [s]*elect* the best candidates. Another example of representative government in action.

GOD'S MANDATE FOR RULERSHIP

Those that serve in civil government, because it is a place of authority, must operate in truth, equity, righteousness and judgment. We are responsible for examining the credentials of persons appointed or elected to positions of authority. If we fail to consider a candidate's position on issues of biblical importance, we subject ourselves to ungodly rule.

When Moses considers the appointment of judges, the scripture plainly indicates men of certain character or reputation were required to fill the office. The candidates must: 1) fear

God; 2) be persons of truth; and 3) not be covetous. Should we, in electing officials today, desire any less?

In Deuteronomy 16:18-19, it is specifically stated: "Judges and officers shalt thou make thee in all thy gates, which the Lord thy God giveth thee, throughout thy tribes and they shall judge the people with just judgment. Thou shalt not wrest judgment; thou shall not respect persons, neither take a gift; for a gift doth blind the eyes of the wise, and pervert the words of the righteous." Truly an ethical directive apropos for today.

In Acts 6, verses 1-5, the people "sought out" men of integrity, full of the spirit of God, and wisdom; these were the required qualifications of "public servants" to fulfill societal obligations to the poor and widows.

God has not changed, he still desires truth, equity, judgment and righteousness in persons who hold positions of authority or sit in high places. The Bible declares that "It is an abomination to kings to commit wickedness; for the throne is established by righteousness."[1] and "The king by judgment establishes the land; but he that receiveth gifts overthroweth it."[2]

THE ABDICATION OF AUTHORITY

God has given man choice. Man is responsible for his choices. Man has an obligation to choose. Man is responsible

---

[1] Proverbs 6:12
[2] Proverbs 29:4

and accountable for his failure to choose. When we refuse to participate in the political process we surrender ground to God's enemies without a fight. We are saying, I am not interested in who rules over my city, state or nation; I am not interested in laws that diminish my freedoms; I am not interested in resisting Satan's agenda for the complete domination of men through wicked policies and practices in the public square.

The Bible states in Ephesians 6:12, "For we wrestle not against flesh and blood but against principalities, against powers, against the rulers of darkness of this world, against spiritual wickedness in high places." As Christians, our adversary can sit in positions of power or "high places." When we fail to be informed and active in the political process we aid and abet the erosion of safeguards designed to usher in blessings of divine providence or favour from Almighty God.

"What safeguards?" you may ask, God ordained principles of righteousness, truth, and equity that result in peace, prosperity and happiness; "Righteousness exalts a nation, but sin is a reproach to any people."[3]

---

[3] Proverbs 14:34

Chapter 2

WHY CHRISTIANS MUST BE POLITICALLY INVOLVED

THE IMPACT OF CHRISTIAN CULTURE

"When the righteous are in authority the people rejoice; when the wicked bear rule, the people mourn." *Proverbs 29:2*

Public policy impacts society. The laws that are made and court decisions that are rendered impact our daily lives either for good or for bad. When the city council votes to allow another liquor license in your neighborhood it opens the door to increased crime and we see the devastating affects of alcohol upon families in our community. When the school board decides that your child has no right to say a prayer over lunch before eating, your religious freedoms are under attack. When the legislature decides that preaching against sin is a hate crime, your right to preach the gospel is being legislated away and will ultimately lead you to a place of decision— whether to obey God or fear what man can do to you. If we are not involved in the daily affairs of the public square, those who don't know God or are anti-Christ have free reign to decide the limits of our liberty. Liberty must be defended in order to be maintained. The source of true liberty is God (where the Spirit of the Lord is there is liberty). The Bible declares that heaven suffers violence, and the violent take it by force. We must be aggressive in praying, fasting and studying God's word for direction on how to live before the world. After we have prayed, fasted and studied, we must take action because faith without works is dead. The survival of our constitutional system depends upon a moral and religious populace. Public acknowledgment of God and His law is essential for a free and moral nation.

Take action: vote, serve on your local city council or school board, become active in the PTA, attend community meetings and public hearings, be informed about the political process, support Christian organizations (that defend our liberties in the public square) with time, finances and prayers; call in to talk shows and advance biblical perspectives.

As a word of caution, the Bible says ...he that wins souls is wise.[4] Use wisdom, the secular world will not listen to you "ranting or raving" about what the Bible says. We must articulate a sound, logical and reasonable argument from a biblical perspective for the position we take on any issue. Jesus was very well versed in the issues of his day. He was able to defeat his enemies by their own words and faulty logic. Know the subject, study the arguments that surround the issue, listen to those that agree and disagree with your position. Arm yourself with the biblical perspective and then stand your ground. We are not called to "argue" in the sense of confusion and strife, for God is not the author of confusion. But we "argue" in the legal sense of the word, taking a position, defending that position with sound doctrine and perhaps persuading some. When the kingdom

---

[4]Proverbs 11:30

of God is advanced through just laws and equitable public policies our entire nation will reap the blessings of God. "Blessed is the nation whose God is the Lord."[5]

<hr>

HISTORICAL CHRISTIAN PARTICIPATION IN POLITICS

Many of the great leaders in our history were ministers of the gospel. African American history is rich in political action. Have we come so far that we have forgotten the cost of our freedom? How can we be so complacent and allow our godly heritage to be stripped away?

The chronicles of history provide evidence that nations that refused God His rightful place in governance have been ruled by tyranny and dictatorship. Russia, China, and Africa, primarily have been ruled by godless governments and human rights have suffered. Edmund Burke said the "The only thing necessary for the triumph of evil, is for good men to do nothing." A garden will grow weeds if left unattended. Jesus said we are a city that is set on a hill that cannot be hid, and if our light be hid, it is hid to them that are lost. We are called to let our light so shine that men will see our good works and glorify our Father in heaven. Men and women who have stood in the face of overwhelming odds armed with truth and faith, have overcome the greatest of obstacles. i.e, Martin Luther King, Jr. (a Republican) was

---

[5]Proverbs 33:12

politically active and he exhibited the Christian value of "be not overcome with evil, but overcome evil with good." American history is replete with ministers of the gospel that used political action to accomplish social good. The "church" in African American history was the center or focal point of the community. Town meetings and political discussions were held there to determine what actions should be taken to liberate men from the bondage of slavery.

Hiram Rhodes Revels, a Senator from Mississippi was born in Fayetteville, Cumberland County, N.C., on September 27, 1827. He attended various schools, seminaries, and Knox College, Galesburg, Ill. He was a barber, an ordained minister in the African Methodist Episcopal Church at Baltimore and elected as a Republican to the United States Senate in 1870.

Richard Harvey Cain, a Representative from South Carolina, entered the ministry, and was a pastor in Brooklyn, N.Y., from 1861 to 1865; he was appointed a bishop of the African Methodist Episcopal Church in 1880; served as a member of the State Senate 1868-1872; and elected as a Republican to the Forty-Third Congress (March 4, 1873-March 3, 1875).

Richard Allen, founder of the AME Church, James Varick organizer of the AME Zion Church, Absalom Jones, founder and organizer of St. Thomas Protestant Episcopal Church were ministers engaged in the fight for the liberty and equality of all men. God did not limit His commission to men only, but utilized the courage and tenacity of women such as Harriet Tubman and Sojourner Truth. Without a moral compass society becomes hedonistic, amoral and immoral. Christians are called to lead by example. Noah Webster, (author of Webster's Dictionary) said, "Let it be impressed on your mind that God commands you to choose for rulers just men who will rule with fear of God. The preservation of a republican government depends on the faithful discharge of this duty; if the citizens neglect their duty and place unprincipled men in office, the government will soon be corrupted."

CULTURAL WARFARE

"Even as they did not like to retain God in their

knowledge, he gave them over to a reprobate mind...."

Romans 1:28

There is a war going on. This war is not new. It is a war of antiquity and it is being fought for the very souls of men. The Bible states that we have an enemy who is wily, cunning, subtle, crafty, scheming, and has the ability to transform himself into an angel of light. Jesus called him the god of this world. Paul tells us to be aware, alert and not ignorant of his devices. But do we really see past individual snares and perceive the danger on a national level?

The warfare is cultural. Satan is working diligently, tirelessly, fearlessly and "in our face" to remove God from the consciousness of America. Prayer has been removed from schools. The Ten Commandments are being removed from courts and public institutions. The phrase "under God" is in jeopardy of being removed from the pledge of allegiance. The preaching against sin, homosexuality in particular, has been criminalized. There is a systematic purging of any mention or public thought of God from society.

We are wrestling against spiritual wickedness in high places as described in Ephesians 6:12. Satan can use people in high places to carry out his anti-God campaign by influencing and possessing the thoughts and wills of men. "High places" are places of authority, i.e., university faculties, public school systems, city councils, assembly/legislatures, congress, courts, police departments, social services departments, hospital boards, the white house, etc. Any position that exercises the power of decision coupled with the authority to enforce that decision is a "high place."

As we sit idly by and allow God to be removed from our national consciousness, we are reaping the harvest of a godless society. Parents are killing their children; children are killing each other; men are lovers of themselves and with themselves; parental authority is being undermined and nullified by court rulings and decisions; there is a push to legalize prostitution and drug use, along with increased pedophilia. Pornography is destroying marriages; greed and corruption are rampant from the lowest levels to the upper echelons of society.

The secularists who believe God has no place in public affairs or society at large are advancing their agenda of removing God from every segment of society. Court case by court case, law by law, public policy by public policy, they are eroding the foundations of freedom in America.

The Supreme Court ruling on the removal of the Ten Commandments from public display is a prime example of the direction in which society is advancing. The Bible says "If the foundations be destroyed, what can the righteous do?"[6] The Ten Commandments are the moral foundation of our law. They summarize the basic principles on which the legal system was based: *respect for life* found in the Commandment "Thou shalt not kill" as the foundation for our homocide statutes; *respect for property* as found in the Commandment "Thou shalt not steal" foundational in our theft and property laws; *respect for truth* found in the Commandment "Thou shalt not bear false witness" and "Thou shalt not take the Name of the Lord thy God in vain" (which prohibits perjury as well as blasphemy); *respect for family* found in the Commandment "Thou shalt not commit adultery" and "Honor thy father and thy mother" as the central role of the

____

[6] Psalms 11:3

family in the legal system being the basic unit of society; *respect for God*, as the source of governmental authority and the source of human rights.

We are allowing the foundations to be destroyed when we fail to join the battle and resist through all means available, particularly the civil process. What will it take to open our eyes and stir us into action?

DEMOCRAT OR REPUBLICAN, DOES IT REALLY MATTER?

A political party consists of a group of people that agree on and vote for particular ideals. Representatives of a political party meet at national conventions every four years and approve a "platform." A platform is a party's "statement of faith." It contains the party's vision, beliefs, values, legislative plan and policy position on important issues of the day. Each position set forth in the platform is called a "plank" and a platform may contain many planks. For example, a party may take a position on education, abortion, homosexuality, prayer in school, etc. and each position or plank forms the platform.

During early American History, the Parties asserted their positions on the issue of slavery. When researching the platforms of the major two parties, Democrats and Republicans, it is interesting to note that while Republicans carried the flag and worked diligently to bring freedom to African Americans, Democrats worked fervently to oppose the Republican's freedom legislation, and used tactics of fear, intimidation, and fraud to keep African Americans from voting. Democrats even went so far as to enact laws that purported white superiority and ultimately used lynching as a means to maintain the "status quo."

It is very sad that many people, particularly African Americans, have no knowledge of political history. Did you know that:

In 1794, Congress banned the exportation of slaves and in 1808, the slave trade was completely banned by Congress.

In 1850, a Democratically controlled Congress passed the Fugitive Slave Law. This law was specifically designed to enable slave owners to recapture slaves. For example, a $10 fee was paid to federal officials who ruled that an African American was a runaway slave, but only $5 if the official ruled the African American was free. Needless to say many free African Americans fled to Canada to escape this new law.

In 1852, Democrats (in their platform) make their position clear, they will resist all attempts and oppose all efforts to abolish slavery.

In 1854, in Ripon, Wisconsin the Republican Party was formed primarily to fight slavery and secure civil rights for African Americans.

In 1857, the US Supreme Court in the Dred Scott decision disregarded the constitutionally authorized ban of 1794 and declared Congress could not interfere with slavery or prohibit it in any territory. This in effect reopened the slave trade.

In 1859, Owen Lovejoy, a white Congressman from Illinois who was the son of a minister, an ordained pastor, and whose brother was murdered by a white pro-slavery mob, delivered a most scathing speech on the House floor against slavery, describing it as a monstrous fanaticism which was maligning the country. In his speech he stated:

> ...twenty-five years ago by universal sentiment the country deemed slavery as a moral, social, and political evil, a wrong to the slave, an injury to the owner, a blight on the soil; slavery was regarded as a hag—ugly, deformed, wrinkled and covered with the daub and paint of harlotry. But now we are told it is an angel of beauty, a virgin decked in bridal attire, to be gazed upon with complacency and love. To have this cancer is no longer a question of being cured, but proclaimed as being sound and the highest type of health. Everyone to enjoy perfect health must have this form of disease gnawing at his vitals. The spirit of this fanaticism has taken possession of the Democratic Party. From the sole of the foot even unto the head, there is no soundness in it; but wounds, and bruises, and putrefying sores; they have not been closed, neither bound up, neither mollified with ointment—unmedicated and unbandaged, it drips with the fetid purescence ....Under what plea was slavery thus allowed to enter in and ravage the heritage of freedom? On the same ground that the madman opens the post-house to let leprosy, plague, and cholera, rush

forth...to walk at midnight and waste at noonday. A man with a contagious disease must not stay in his own house, nor be confined in the hospital; but must be allowed to roam abroad, to spread disease and death among his fellowman...But the strangest and most impious phase of this fanaticism is, that it claims the sanction of the Bible for American slavery....as for the grand old Hebrew, in which the ancient Scriptures were written, it has no word which describes or recognizes a human being as a piece of property...if the Bible sanctions slavery at all, it is the enslavement of white men. No one pretends that the servants spoken of in the Bible were blacks. The Roman slave was not a black man, the Hebrew servant was not a black man, the question is, whether the laboring man, white or black, may rightfully be enslaved? I may as well notice, here, that worn-out question erroneously placed on Ham. Noah planted a vineyard, raise some grapes, made some wine and got drunk. When he waked up, still fuddled with the fornea of the wine...so confused he did not know his son from his grandson, he uttered the malediction, "cursed be Cannan," not Ham, who had been guilty of the wrong. Now in the blaze of the nineteen century, with the radians of Christianity shining around, Democrats go mousing back five thousand years to learn the basis of human rights from the lips of a man still half drunk. "Cursed be Cannan," is evermore the refrain of the Democratic minstrelay...And now to the Bible. I will not detain the committee long, for I have no patience with the impiety that attempts to throw the sanction of this holy book around the diabolical system of American slavery...What says this inspired volume? "Thou shalt not steal!" Brief, comprehensive and to the point. This must be taken from the Bible before it can be made to sanction slavery...The title to every slave originated in violence and robbery, and its continuance has no other moral character. There can be no mistake about the rightful ownership of a human being. He belongs to himself....But we have a specific statute on this subject "He that stealeth a man and selleth him, or if he be found in his hands," that is, in his possession, "he shall surely be put to death." This enactment takes this transaction out of the catalogue of ordinary crime and brands it with peculiar reprobation...Honor thy father and thy mother, is the requirement of the Bible. Slavery utterly annuls this command. The owner claims honor and obedience, to the utter disregard of parental authority and parental claims. Whoever thinks of a slave child obeying his parent in preference to his master? The very suggestion is preposterous. Does the Bible sanction a system that abrogates its own injunction? There stands that slave mother, pressing with a mother's love, her own child to her heart! To whom does it belong? Is it not hers against the universe? Is there any being, this side of the throne of God, that has the right to take it from her? Has the master the right to come and tear it away from her embraces, and claim it as his property? And is this robbery sanctioned by the Bible, and that Bible the word of God?...These men do not truly interpret the Bible. They teach for doctrines the commandments of men, and make the word of

God of none effect through their traditions. How dare these men make the Bible lend its sanction to a system that abrogates parental authority and filial duty. So also with the conjugal relation. The Bible everywhere represents this as the most sacred, inviolate, and indissoluble of all human relations. Father and mother are to be forsaken in obedience to the claims of this still higher and holier relation. Now what does slavery do with this domestic institution? Leave God and the parties perfectly free to regulate it in their own way? No! With impious and brazen front, it steps in and utterly annihilates the marriage relation so far as its victims are concerned. There is no more any legal marriage among the three or four million slaves in the United States than there is among so many cattle...Would it not be an interesting spectacle to see one of these clergyman who teach that the Bible sanctions slavery, called in to attend the wedding of a bureau and chest of drawers? The chairs, and shovel, and tongs, are invited as guests. There can be no more a legal marriage between two slaves, than between two articles of furniture. The Bible says: "what God hath joined together, let not man put asunder." The slave systems says: Who cares for God? I will separate them when I please...It can truly be said of slavery, that there is nothing that it does not touch, and nothing that it does not defile. It has perverted the Government, violated the national faith, muzzled the press, debauched the church, corrupted Christianity, and seeks to change the glory of the invisible God and into a Moloch, and transform the eternal and loving Father in to a patron of cruelty, lust, and injustice, and then with the impudence of the strange woman, wipes its mouth and says, "I have committed no sin!" I should be ashamed of such a God as that. It is to me utterly incomprehensive, that any one can sincerely believe that the Bible sanctions the system of American slavery; and I leave that point...

In 1859, John Brown influenced by his father who was strongly opposed to slavery and assisted in the Underground Railroad, formed the United States League of Gileadites to resist slave-catchers. He led an attack on the federal armory at Harper's Ferry in hopes of encouraging slaves to join the rebellion. John Brown was captured, tried and convicted of insurrection, treason and murder. He was executed. A song was written, John Brown's Body, to remember the valiant raid on Harper's Ferry, and was played as a marching tune by Republican soldiers during the war.

In 1860, Democrats supported the 1857 Dred Scott decision declaring African Americans were not persons but property. The decision said African Americans had no rights, which the white man was bound to respect, and that the Negro might justly and lawfully be reduced to slavery for his own benefit. Democrats were viciously opposed to Republicans, and Repesentative T.C. Hindman of Arkansas, (a Democrat) gave a vitriolic speech on the floor of the House of Representatives denouncing the Republican Party's candidate for Speakership:

The party opposed to us was, and is, that known as Republican—a title synonymous in our estimation, with sectionalism, with hostility to State rights, with disloyalty to the Constitution, with treason to the Government, and with civil war, bloodshed, murder, and rapine. That it is a sectional party is shown by the fact that it has no representative here except from the northern States, and that it sprang to life out of the festering prejudices of northern anti-slavery malignity, and is kept alive by appeals to those prejudices only. That it is hostile to State rights, and disloyal to the Constitution, is shown by its openly avowed intention to keep the leading property interest of the South out of the common Territories, by congressional prohibition of slavery there, which the Supreme Court of the Union has solemnly adjudged to be unconstitutional. That it is a treasonable party is shown by its nullification of the fugitive slave law, in at least eight northern States, and its persistent refusal to comply with the Federal compact for the delivering up of fugitive slaves. Not only is this done in that number of States, but constant efforts are made to add to the black list of recreant and dishonored sovereignties...Let the civilized world judge between the slaveholders of the South, who hold the negro in that subordination for which nature and nature's God intended him, and the false philanthropists of the North, who inflict, or consent to the infliction, on white man and women, of such intolerable outrages and grievances...I said that the tenants and practices of the Republican party lead to civil war, to bloodshed, to murder, and to rapine. That is shown by John Brown's invasions of Virginia, and slaughter of her peaceable citizens. The Republican members here may now disclaim all sympathy with that old traitor; they may say again and again that they contributed nothing to his enterprise, either in men, money, arms, or favorable wishes; but until they shall have abandoned Republicanism, and repented their connection with it, a discerning and intelligent-public will deride and spare all such protestations. The innocent lambs that now bleat so gently, under fear of popular condemnation, are the same men who wrought up the northern mind to that pitch of frenzy out of which John Brown's bloody raid proceeded. By their maddening and furious abuse of slavery and slaveholders, they set on fire the brain of that old fanatic. Had there been no Republican party, there would have been no invasion of Harper's Ferry. John Brown was the tool of republicanism, doing its work; and now, that work is done, Republican politicians cannot skulk the responsibility. The country will hold them to it and will gibbet them for it, as effectually as if the hemp that strangled John Brown and his confederates had also strangled these his instigators, from SEWARD, the author of the infamous irreprehensible-conflict doctrine, down to the last made convert and disciple, the member from Pennsylvania [laughter on the Democratic side] I refer to that member from Pennsylvania [Mr. Hickman] who has on this floor twice threatened to apply the teaching of SEWARD, and to reenact the conduct of John Brown, by mustering and marching eighteen million northern men against the South, to whip her into submission to the higher law. When that invasion is made, the price of hemp will go up, for our whole crop will be needed to hang the Abolition soldiery; [laughter from Democrats and the galleries] but the price of arms will go down, for we will take from our invaders arms enough to equip our whole populations [applause from Democratic benches and the galleries]. The history of that invasion will be like that of the old Assyrian raid into Judea; the fate of its forces will be the same as that of the hosts of Sennacherib...That sir, will be the fate of the invaders of southern soil. In the language of a prominent Republican member of this House, "we will welcome them with bloody hands, to hospitable graves" [applause in the galleries]. This traitorous, sectional, and bloody Republican party is the one that met us at the threshold of this House..not content to rely upon its abominable record..it presented a candidate with a still more abominable record of his own; thus adding to our sense of injury the galling consciousness of intended insult. That candidate has repeatedly referred us and the country to his congressional record here, as the index to his opinions on the great question of the day and announces his willingness to be judged by that test....he insists upon the exclusion of slavery from certain territory by congressional legislation; and then he declares that new slaveholding States shall not be admitted into the Confederacy. At one time he brands the fugitive slave act as "a savage and inhuman law;" then he stigmatizes slavery as "an injury to the master and a crime against the slave." And finally giving full scope and vent to his abolition zeal, he becomes a practical encourager of negro-stealing, and an assistant of the underground railroad. I think, the attitude held by Mr. Sherman on the subject of negro stealing...for the punishment of that crime, pure and simple, he would give no aid. The agents of the underground railroad might ply their trade and go scot free, so far as he was concerned. Stealing slaves and taking them abolitionward was, in his view, a philanthropic enterprise, not only not to be punished, but to be shielded by non-legislation and sheltered by well-put parliamentary objections. But when it appears that the thieves have strong pro-slavery proclivities; that they are "sound on the nigger question," and carry their spoils, not North, but South, to put them in southern cotton fields, instead of translating them to the mock freedom of non-slaveholding States; then the position of the member from Ohio changes: the action is reversed, and his objections with withdrawn. A pro-slavery negro thief must be punished by all means. To that there is no objections. Oh! no sir. But an anti-slavery negro thief must not be molested. This is one of the beauties of the record on which the Republican candidate so complacently plumes himself...Sewardism, Helperism, and Shermanism are identical. The black mantle of Republicanism covers them all....I charge the gentleman with having previously advocated upon this floor the exclusion of slavery, by congressional legislation, from certain Territories, I charge him with having avowed his intention to oppose the admission of new slaveholding States into this Confederacy. I have charged him with having branded the fugitive slave law, an act based upon the Constitution of this country, as a savage and inhuman law. I charged him with having

stigmatized a domestic institution of the southern
States of the Union as an injury to the master
and a crime against the slave. Those matters are
yet to be met by the gentleman, and I call his
attention to them.

Mr. Sherman responded: I am charged with being
a Republican. That is my offense; none other.

In 1862, General David Hunter, like General Fremont, not only enlisted African American soldiers, but issued a statement freeing all slaves in Georgia, South Carolina, and Florida. President Lincoln demanded a retraction and the disbandment of the First South Carolina regiment.

In 1863, President Lincoln issued the Emancipation Proclamation. Initially Lincoln refused the admittance of African Americans into the army and returned fugitive slaves to slave holders. When General John C. Fremont issued a proclamation freeing slaves in Missouri in August 1861, Lincoln revoked the proclamation and relieved General Fremont of his command. There were letters written in support of Fremont because he was popular with the Radical Republicans and a founding member of the Republican Party. Lincoln's position was to save the Union, not to save or destroy slavery. He wanted to deport all African Americans to a black settlement somewhere in Central America. When it became clear that African Americans, upon proving their bravery in battle, were needed to win the war then President Lincoln finalized the Emancipation Proclamation which he drafted in July 22, 1862, and claimed that he would free all slaves in those states in rebellion on January 1, 1863.

In 1864, A Republican Congress passed the 13th Amendment to the Constitution abolishing slavery; slave holding states (Southern Democrats) seceded from the Union and the Confederacy was established.

In 1865, Congress established the Freedman's Bureau. The Freeman's Bureau established schools, hospitals, houses and food supplies for freed slaves. Senator Charles Sumner, a Radical Republican, presented a bill to the Joint Committee on Reconstruction requesting land for the settlement of African Americans freed by war and proclamation of the President of the United States. The order granted a plot of not more than 40 acres of tillable ground and military protection until the newly freed slaves could protect themselves or until Congress finalized the land deeds. Senator Charles Sumner, because of his passionate opposition to slavery, was brutally attacked while seated at his desk in the Senate by a Southern Carolina Congressman, Preston S. Brooks. Sumner was attacked because of his "Crime against Kansas" speech which opposed the extending of slavery into Kansas. This attack became known as the infamous "Caning of Senator Charles Sumner."

In 1866, the 14th Amendment to the Constitution was proposed (and subsequently passed in 1868) which included language that defined an American citizen as anyone born in the US or naturalized, automatically making African Americans citizens.

The passage of the 14th and 15th Amendments to the US Constitution is credited to the effects of Radical Republicans. There were two types of Republicans, moderates and radicals. The Radical Republicans were of the opinion that no Southern state should be readmitted to the Union until African Americans were treated equally in law and practice. Representative Thaddeus Stevens, a Radical Republican, was strongly in favor of taking land away from slave owners and in a one speech stated:

> We have turned, or are about to turn, loose four million slaves without a hut to shelter them or a cent in their pockets. The infernal laws of slavery have prevented them from acquiring an education, understanding of the common laws of contract, or of managing the ordinary business of life. This Congress is bound to provide for them until they can take are of themselves. If we do not furnish them with homesteads, and hedge them around with protective laws; if we leave them to the legislation of their late masters, we had better have left them in bondage.

Land (40 acres) that had been given in good faith to freed men was returned to the slave masters by Democrat President Andrew Johnson. Thaddeus Stevens was so committed to the African American cause that his epitaph read: "I repose in this quiet and secluded spot, not from any natural preference for solitude, but, finding, other cemeteries limited by charter rules as to race, I have chosen this, that I might illustrate in my death the principles which I advocated through a long life—Equality of Man before his Creator."

In 1866, Major General Rufus Saxton, a Freedman's Bureau assistant commissioner, testified before Congress on his assessment of the freed slaves aspirations regarding land ownership. Saxton testified that freed slaves mostly desired to purchase land but former slave owners had a policy to prevent freed slaves from becoming landholders. It was the desire of former slaveholders to keep the newly freed slaves in a condition as near to slavery as possible. However, if the freed slave was given possession of all the rights of citizenship, they would advance rapidly. The most intelligent freedmen were loyal to the Republican Party. General Saxton testified that for the prosperity of the two races in the south, freed men should immediately be put into possession of all rights and that the word color should be left out of all laws, constitutions, and regulations as necessary for the vital safety of the Union.

In 1867, under military control, authorized elections allowed all males (irrespective of color) to vote. Black voters outnumbered whites in many Democratic southern states. Freed slaves with the right of political access, voting power, were a threat to the Democrat Party because African Americans were being elected to state and national offices and elected Republican candidates.

As former slaves were elected to political office it was embarrassing to the former slave owners that these newly freed slaves were adept in functioning within the political sphere. Seeing this, the slave owners had to subjugate these "freed men" another way. Hence, a paramilitary organization was formed known as the Klu Klux Klan. **The primary purpose of the Klan was to reduce the African American to political impotence** through stealth, murder, economic intimidation, political assassinations, political terror and through raw fear.

By 1868, the Republicans had abolished slavery and passed laws repealing the Fugitive Slave Act. The Democrat Party platform demanded the abolition of all political instruments designed to secure Negro supremacy. The first Grand Wizard of the Ku Klux Klan was Democrat Nathan Bedford Forrest, an honoree at the Democratic National Convention.

In 1869, Congress introduced the 15th Amendment prohibiting the denial of voting rights based on race, color, or previous conditions of servitude. This Amendment was ratified in 1870.

In 1871, the Klu Klux Klan Act was passed by Congress and no Democrat voted to support this legislation calling for the punishment of Klan violence.

In 1875, Republicans passed civil rights legislation to prohibit segregation and racial discrimination. Not one Democrat voted for the bill. Democrats successfully blocked any further civil rights progress until the mid-1960s. Republicans lost their majority in Congress and the Democrat Party gained control of Congress, the era of advancement for African Americans came to a halt.

In 1876, Democrats enacted a litany of deterrents to bar African Americans from participating in the political process. Deterrents included poll taxes, literacy tests, grandfather clauses, multiple ballots, hide and seek polling places, Black Codes (Jim Crow laws), forced segregation, white only primaries, property ownership requirements, and annual voter registration fees.

In 1884, the Republican Party, in their platform, expressed their unalterable opposition to servile labor. (One form of servile labor was instituted through "Black Codes" which created criminal offenses for minor charges such as vagrancy, insubordination, disrespect, and other verbal offenses). An African American convicted of such a crime was sent into plantation labor, in essence, returned to slavery.

In1888, Representative John Roy Lynch was deprived of his seat in Congress (Sixth District of Mississippi) because of voter fraud by the Democrat Party. According to Representative Lynch, "More colored than white men are thus persecuted simply because they constitute in larger numbers the opposition to the Democratic Party." U.S. Representative Richard Cain of South Carolina, a Bishop of the AME denomination agreed, declaring "The bad blood of the South comes because the Negros are Republicans. If they would only cease to be Republicans and vote the straight-out Democratic ticket there would be no trouble. Then the bad blood would sink entirely out of sight."

In 1892, the Republican Party platform calls for every citizen of the United States to be allowed to cast one free and unrestricted ballot in all public elections, and the enactment of laws to enforce and secure every citizen, rich or poor, native or foreign-born, black or white as guaranteed by the U.S. Constitution. The Democrats answered this call with voter intimidation.

In 1892, there were 70,000 more blacks than whites in Mississippi; but white voters outnumbered blacks by a margin of 8 to 1. In Alabama, the number of black voters was reduced from 181,000 in 1901 to only 3,000 by 1902; in Texas from 100,000 in 1890s to only 5,000 by 1906. In 1965, in Selma, Alabama, a city with more black residents than whites, the voting rolls were 99 percent white and 1 percent black. The Democrat voter suppression efforts were effective.

Isn't it interesting that so many lives were destroyed over the issue of voting and today with all the freedoms and conveniences of voting (absentee), as a whole, African Americans are the least represented in the electoral process. Not only do we fail to vote consistently, we fail to vote INFORMED.

In 1893, the Democrat Party took control of the Presidency, and both houses of Congress.

By 1895, the Democrats had succeeded in repealing most of the civil rights legislation enacted during the post civil war period under the Republicans. African Americans were completely at the mercy of southern state governments, all of which were controlled by Democrats. No civil rights legislation was passed between 1892 and 1964. Isn't it strange the Democrats pretend to be the party of "civil rights" when in fact as history reveals, they were committed to keeping African Americans from gaining equality in American society?

By 1900, Democrats began actively seeking a repeal of the 15th Amendment. U.S. Senator Ben Tillman from South Carolina, states the Democrat Party has made up its mind that the 14th and 15th Amendments to the Constitution were null and void, calling the 15th Amendment the political blunder of the century.

In 1908, the Republican Party Platform continued it support by proclaiming its consistent friendship of the African American for more than fifty years and demanded equal justice for all men without regard to race or color. The platform reiterated without reservation the enforcement of the letter and spirit of the 14th and 15th Amendments as designed for the protection and advancement of the African Americans. The platform condemned all devices aimed at disfranchisement based upon color alone as unfair, un-American and repugnant to the supreme law of the land.

In 1920, the Republican Party Platform called for Congress to consider the most effective means to end lynching which continued to be a terrible blot on the American civilization.

In 1921, US Rep. Leonidas Dyer of Missouri introduced a federal anti-lynching bill, Democrats fought its passage and eventually killed the bill.

It was not until the 1940's that the Democrat party begin making overtures of inclusion through equality language in their platforms. While Franklin D. Roosevelt initiated the conversation, Harry S. Truman was the first Democrat President to advocate for strong civil rights protection. He proposed an anti-lynching law, a ban on poll taxes, and desegregation of the military. Unfortunately, the Democrat Congress killed those proposals along with the proposed Civil Rights Commission. Even during the 1950's and 60's, it was the Democrat Party that opposed integration of the public school system. It was a Republican President who sent federal troops to protect African American children during desegregation in southern states. Only a few Democrat Governors supported integrating the public school system.

In 1964, the infamous Civil Rights Act, which was originally drafted by President Eisenhower in 1957, was submitted by a Democrat President, Lyndon B. Johnson. The Act was fiercely opposed by the Democrat Party through extended and lengthy filibusters. Even though the Democrats had 315 members in Congress (almost 2/3 of the House and 2/3 of the Senate) only 219 votes (a majority) were needed to pass the bill. 198 Democrats voted to pass the Act. If Republicans had not supported the 1964 Civil Rights Act and the 1965 Voting Rights Act, the legislation would have failed to become law.

Historically, African Americans were loyal to the Republican Party. The first African Americans to be elected to political office were Republicans. In 1875, U.S. Representative Joseph Hayne Rainey said "We intend to continue to vote so long as the government gives us the right and necessary protection; and I know that right accorded to us now will never be withheld in the future if left to the Republican Party." The first African American Senator to be elected to Congress as a Democrat was Carol Moseley-Braun in 1992. The first African American Republicans elected to public office included:

Pinckney Benton Stewart Pinchback (May 10, 1837 – December 21, 1921). The first African-American to become governor of a U.S. State. He was elected to the Louisiana state senate in 1868, and became its president pro tempore. Upon the death of Oscar Dunn, the lieutenant governor of Louisiana, Pinchback became lieutenant governor in 1871. From Dec. 9, 1872, to Jan. 13, 1873, he served as acting governor while impeachment proceedings were in progress against Henry Clay Warmoth. In 1872, Pinchback was elected to Congress, but his Democratic opponent contested the election and won the seat. A year later he was elected to the

U.S. Senate, but he was again refused the seat amid charges and countercharges of fraud and election irregularities. Pinchback eventually moved to New York City where he was a Federal Marshall, and then to Washington, D.C. where he practiced law.

Blanche Kelso Bruce, a Senator from Mississippi was born in slavery near Farmville, Prince Edward County, Va., March 1, 1841. He was elected as a Republican to the United States Senate and served from March 4, 1875 to March 3, 1881. He was the first African American to serve a full term in the United States Senate, and was appointed Register of the Treasury by President James Garfield 1881.

Joseph Hayne Rainey, a Representative from South Carolina was born in Georgetown, Georgetown County, S.C., June 21, 1832. He was a delegate to the State constitutional convention in 1868 and became a member of the State senate in 1870 but resigned. He was then elected as a Republican to the Forty-First Congress to fill the vacancy caused by the action of the House of Representatives in declaring the seat of B. Franklin

Whittemore vacant and was the first African American to be elected to the House of Representatives. Rainey was reelected to the Forty-Second and three succeeding Congresses, serving from December 12, 1870 to March 3, 1879. Joseph Hayne Rainey was appointed an internal-revenue agent of South Carolina on May 22, 1879, and served until July 15, 1881, when he resigned.

Justice Jonathan Jasper Wright was born in 1840. He was the first African American Supreme Court Justice, elected to South Carolina Supreme Court February 1, 1870, and served until his resignation December 1, 1877.

Edward William Brooke, III, a Senator from Massachusetts, born in Washington, D.C., on October 26, 1919. He was elected attorney general of the Commonwealth of Massachusetts in 1962, reelected in 1964, and elected to the United States Senate in 1966. He was reelected in 1972 and served from January 3, 1967, to January 3, 1979. Edward William Brooke, III was the first African American elected to the Senate by popular vote.

The Republicans have a rich history of supporting African Americans. Were it not for the Republican Party the 13th, 14th, and 15th Amendments to the Constitution would not have been passed. In 1874, the Great Compromise, which gave Rutherford Hayes the presidency, began the decline of Republican power. The agreement exchanged the presidency for withdrawal of federal troops from southern states. These federal troops were for the protection of African American voters. When African Americans' voting rights were left unprotected, the Republican Party lost power and the southern Democrats regained Congress. It was the Democrats that burned African American schools and churches to prevent the education of the "Negro." Democrats have used scare tactics to keep African American voters on their plantation by suggesting that African Americans could lose their voting rights if the 1965 Voting Rights Act were to expire or sunset. This is bogus. The Voting Rights Act of 1965 had to be enacted to enforce the 15th Amendment to the U.S. Constitution passed by the Republicans in 1869. It was the Democrat Party that opposed African American participation in the political process. How hypocritical. Through economic allurements (welfare) African Americans began to abandon the Republican Party and return to the economic slavery of the Democrat Party. Isn't it amazing that welfare as passed in the early sixties required the family to become fatherless in order to qualify for "subsidies?" Families were torn apart by sheer brutal force during the 1800s, in the

1960s the Democrats found a new way to keep African American families divided—welfare.

In 1961 the United States Commission on Civil Rights conducted several studies on the status of Black America. One of the studies was on African American participation in voting. Some of the conclusions were very interesting and are still applicable today.

Then: Discrimination inhibited voting. Overt as well as subtle inhibitions were utilized as a means for exclusion. Fear of physical or economic reprisal was very effective, educated African Americans were warned to refrain from taking too active an interest in political matters lest they lose their jobs or their lives. Without exception African Americans as a political entity were ignored and purposely encouraged to keep a passive place. A crucial conclusion drawn from the study is the fact that economics had a direct and significant impact on civil rights generally and on voting in particular.

Now: The poorer you are the less likely you are to participate in the political process. (Now who works the hardest at keeping us financially destitute and on welfare? Do we really think welfare is in our best interest?) Another major contributor to non-voting among African Americans is apathy.

Then and Now: The history of exclusion from full citizenship continues to control [the Negros] our actions even after the acts of exclusion have ceased. Other factors that contribute to low [Negro] voter registration appears to be low level of education. (Ever wonder why your high schooler is graduating without the ability to read at even the eighth grade level? Do you think this is by accident?)

Isn't it interesting that the political party that opposed "Negro" participation in the electoral process in the 1800s is the same political party that dominates the welfare and public education systems of today?

With that bit of history laid on the table, let's address the political party positions of today in light of a Biblical perspective: (The following are positions taken by the Republican and Democrat Parties as indicated in their party platforms in 2004).

Biblical Position: Proverbs 22:6
Train up a child in the way he should go; and when he is old, he will not depart from it.

Republican Party:	Democrat Party:
Support prayer in school, parental involvement in the education of their children, and school choice. *"We will continue to work for the return of volunteer school prayer. We support the use of faith-based organizations. We applaud efforts to promote school choice initiatives that give parents more control."*	No mention of prayer in school; oppose school vouchers which would provide choice to parent in educating their children *"Instead of supporting vouchers we will support public school choice."* (Isn't it interesting that Democrats scream for "choice" except where choice will reduce their control; public school choice is no choice at all.)

Biblical Position: Psalm 127:3; Psalms 106:37-38
Lo, children are an heritage of the Lord; and the fruit of the womb is his reward.

Yea, they sacrificed their sons and their daughters unto devils, and shed innocent blood, even the blood of their sons and of their daughters, whom they sacrificed unto the idols of Canaan; and the land was polluted with blood.

Republican Party:	Democrat Party:
Opposes abortion, partial birth abortion, and supports the position that life begins at conception. *"The unborn child has a fundamental individual right to life which cannot be infringed. We oppose using public revenues for abortion and will not fund organizations which advocate it."*	Supports a "woman's right to choose" (an euphemism for abortion), partial birth abortion (where the baby is pulled out of the birth canal breach while leaving the head in the canal and having scissors plunged into its head to collapse the head and suck out the brains). *"We stand proudly for a woman's right to choose, consistent with Roe v. Wade, and regardless of ability to pay."*

Biblical Position: Romans 1:26-27; Leviticus 18:22

For this cause God gave them up unto vile affections: for even their women did change the natural use into that which is against nature: And likewise also the men, leaving the natural use of the woman, burned in their lust one toward another; men with men working that which is unseemly, and receiving in themselves that recompence of their error which was meet.

Thou shalt not lie with mankind, as with womankind; it is abomination.

Republican Party:	Democrat Party:
Opposes the homosexual lifestyle. *"Homosexuality is incompatible with military service."*	Supports gay, lesbian, transgender, transsexual lifestyles as the norm and forces their abnormal views upon society by creating new protected class(es). *"We will enact bipartisan legislation barring workplace discrimination based on sexual orientation."*

Biblical Position: Genesis 2:24

Therefore shall a man leave his father and his mother, and shall cleave unto his wife: and they shall be one flesh.

Republican Party:	Democrat Party:
Supports marriage as between one man and one woman; *"We call for a Constitutional amendment that fully protects marriage, and we believe that neither federal nor state judges should force states to recognize other living arrangements as equivalent to marriage."*	Supports alternate lifestyles *"We support the full inclusion of gay and lesbian families in the life of the nation and seek equal responsibilities, benefits, and protections of these families."*

These platforms while representing the Party positions, do not speak specifically to the issue of euthanasia. However, consistent with recent public debate and the belief that life is sacred, I would venture to say the Republican Party opposes doctor assisted suicide or euthanasia; while the Democrat Party supports "an individual's right" to end their life.

Democrat or Republican, does it really matter?

<hr>

DON'T VOTE THE STATUS QUO

Why do we, particularly African Americans, continue to vote with blind loyalty to a party that exploits our socio-economic status? Why do we, particularly African Americans, aid and abet the anti-God movement by supporting candidates and legislation that advance the secular humanist agenda? Why do we vote contrary to what we claim we believe in, biblical principles and family values. Do we really understand the political position we take (voting or not voting) is a statement about us as a culture? Stop being led like sheep to the slaughter. Ask questions, know what you are voting for and why. Look beyond the short-term "gains" and examine the long-term implications of your vote.

Voting is power. Conventional voting studies say that most voters are: 1) not well informed; 2) apathetic if not cynical; 3) inclined to vote as their parents did; 4) inclined to vote as members of their social groups have previously done; and 5) inclined to be somewhat less than rational in their decision processes and choices.

Alexis de Tocqueville said "One of the most ordinary weaknesses of the human intellect is to seek to reconcile contrary principles and to purchase peace at the expense of logic."

Chapter 3

IS SEPARATION OF CHURCH AND STATE A VALID EXCUSE?

Separation of church and state. A phrase that has become the battlecry of those who oppose the active participation and acknowledgment of religion in the public square. Christians have used this phrase as an excuse to justify their refusal to participate in the political process. But where did this phrase come from? Is it in the constitution? Who said it and why?

In 1947, in the case *Everson* v. *Board of Education*, the Supreme Court declared, "The First Amendment has erected a wall between church and state. That wall must be kept high and impregnable. We could not approve the slightest breach." The "separation of church and state" phrase which they invoked, and which has today become so familiar, was taken from an exchange of letters between President Thomas Jefferson and the Baptist Association of Danbury, Connecticut, shortly after Jefferson became President.

In a letter dated October 7, 1801, the Danbury Baptists expressed to President Jefferson their grave concerns regarding the First Amendment which guaranteed the free exercise of religion.

> "Our sentiments are uniformly on the side of religious liberty; that Religion is at all times and places a matter between God and individuals, that no man ought to suffer in name, person, or effects on account of his religious opinions, [and] that the legitimate power

of civil government extends no further than to punish the man who works ill to his neighbor. But sir, our constitution of government is not specific. Our ancient charter, together with the laws made coincident therewith, were adapted as the basis of our government at the time of our revolution. And these favors we receive at the expense of such degrading acknowledgments, as are inconsistent with the rights of freemen. It is not to be wondered at therefore, if those who seek after power and gain, under the pretense of government and Religion, should reproach their fellow men, [or] should reproach their Chief magistrate, as an enemy of religion, law, and good order, because he will not, dares not, assume the prerogative of Jehovah and make laws to govern the Kingdom of Christ.

Sir, we are sensible that the President of the United States is not the National Legislator and also sensible that the national government cannot destroy the laws of each State, but our hopes are strong that the sentiment of our beloved President, which have had such genial effect already, like the radiant beams of the sun, will shine and prevail through all these States - and all the world - until hierarchy and tyranny be destroyed from the earth. Sir, when we reflect on your past services and see a glow of philanthropy and goodwill shining forth in a course of more than thirty years, we have reason to believe that America's God has raised you up to fill the Chair of State out of that goodwill which he bears to the millions which you preside over. May God strengthen you for the arduous task which providence and the voice of the people have called you - to sustain and support you and your Administration against all the predetermined opposition of those who wish to rise to wealth and importance on the poverty and subjection of the people.

May the Lord preserve you safe from every evil and bring you at last to his Heavenly Kingdom through Jesus Christ our Glorious Mediator."[7]

In other words, the inclusion of protection for the exercise of religion in the constitution suggested that the right of religious expression was man/government (alienable) given rather than God-given (inalienable); and someday the government might attempt to regulate religious expression.

President Jefferson believed that the First Amendment language guaranteeing the "free exercise of religion" was to prevent the establishment of a national denomination. He was a strong proponent of this position and in his reply to the Danbury Baptists on January 1, 1802, he wrote:

"Gentlemen, the affectionate sentiment of esteem and approbation which you are so good as to express towards me, on behalf of the Danbury Baptist Association, give me the highest satisfaction...Believe with you that religion is a matter which lies solely between man and his God, that he owes account to none other for his faith or his worship, that the legislative powers of government reach actions only, and not opinions,

I contemplate with sovereign reverence that act of the whole American people which declared that their legislature would "make no law respecting an establishment or religion, or prohibiting the free exercise thereof," thus building a wall of separation between Church and State. Adhering to this expression of the supreme will of the nation in behalf of the rights of conscience, I shall see with sincere satisfaction the progress of those sentiments which tend to restore to man all his natural rights, convinced he has no natural right in opposition to his social duties. I reciprocate your kind prayers for the protection and blessing of the common Father and Creator of man, and tender you for yourselves and your religious association, assurances of my high respect and esteem."

President Jefferson believed that because God was the author and source of our rights, the government would be barred from interference with those rights. The "wall" of the Danbury letter was NOT to limit religious activities in the public square, but to limit the power of government to prohibit or interfere with the free expression of religious rights.

It was not until 1947, did a court take the words of this private letter out of context and use it to strike down state laws which encourage or facilitate public religious expressions. Prior to the mis-use of the "separation of church and state" concept, courts had interpreted the phrase correctly in that only when activities violated social duties of good order (i.e., human sacrifice, polygamy, bigamy, incest, infanticide, parricide, etc.) under the guise of religion did the government have a legitimate reason to become involved. Let's stop perpetuating the fallacy of an erroneous interpretation.

———————●———————

GOD'S MANDATE FOR SOCIAL REFORM

"The wicked shall be turned into hell, and all nations that forget God." *Psalms 9:17*

God's requirements for a healthy and happy society has not changed. God still demands individual responsibility and accountability. To each of us has been given the ability to be reconciled into relationship with Him through His Son, Jesus Christ. Society's socio-economic policies must come from a "love thy neighbor as thyself" philosophy. Without the true originator and source of love, this will never occur; for the heart of man is deceitful above all and desperately wicked.[1] Only when man recognizes his sinful state and acknowledges his need for a Savior (realizing that without God he is destined for destruction) will transformation occur. God is the source of liberty, justice, happiness, peace, and prosperity. Without God involved in the affairs of man, man's attempt at social reform is futile. Moral behavior, self restraint, love for one's neighbor as one's self, all

---

[1] Jeremiah 17:9

being necessities for a civil society, originate with one's relationship with God. Social reform is first individual and then collective.

THE OSTRICH SYNDROME

"Therefore to him that knoweth to do good and doeth it not, to him it is sin." *James 4:17*

Some say "I don't want to get involved"; others say "it makes no difference they are going to do what they want anyway;" "God is in control and whatever He wants to happen will, no matter what we do." There are sins of commission and sins of omission. Apathy and fatalism are devices of the enemy. If you are distracted, diverted and sitting idly on the sidelines, you are no threat to the enemy's kingdom. J.C. Ryle, in Walking with God, said:

> "Separation from the world does not mean that Christians should take no interest in anything except religion. Some may think it very spiritual to neglect science, art, literature, and politics, to read no books except spiritual ones, to read no newspapers and to know nothing about the government of their country. I think that is an idle and selfish neglect of duty. [Apostle] Paul valued good government (I Tim. 2:1-2); he knew the law and customs of the world. Christians who pride themselves on ignorance bring religion into contempt."

When we engage first and foremost the weapons of our warfare: prayer, fasting, and knowledge of our God, then we can engage the enemy. If not you, then who?

First they came for the Jews, and I did not speak out because I was not a Jew. Then they came for the communists, and I did not speak out because I was not a communist. Then they came for the trade unionist, and I did not speak out because I was not a trade unionist. Then they came for me and there was no one left to speak out for me."

Martin Niemöller 1945

Chapter 4

RULES OF ENGAGEMENT

REGISTER TO VOTE

There are those of us, particularly the African American community, that tend to bemoan the state of affairs but rarely take action to change the situation; stop talking and start acting. You can make a difference. Voting is a right that was paid for by blood, sweat, and tears. Those who have died for the right to participate in the political process would "turn over in their graves" to know we have become distracted, apathetic, disenchanted and give up so easily. Being registered to vote says, I care about my neighbor, my community, my state and my nation. Failing to register or to vote gives you no right to bemoan or lament the state of affairs of the nation. What are you doing to change the situation? Faith without works is dead. Show me your faith without your works and I will show you my faith by my works. Faith is not just some ethereal phantom, it is a word that requires we actively do something about what we believe.

————●————

PRAY, READ, ACT

It has been said in times past, if you want to hide things from black folks, just write it in a book. Times certainly have changed, but we have yet to practice what we have learned. Current affairs are readily available through newspapers, online news, television, radio, etc. But how much consideration do we actually give to disturbing trends in our society?

The Bible says that men ought to always pray and not to faint. Faint means to give up, to get so discouraged that you quit, to literally let the devil win. In the book of Matthew, Jesus says to watch and pray that we enter not into temptation. But somewhere along the way our eyes have become heavy and we no longer are watching. When you hear of murders, rapes or molestations, robberies, drug busts, or corporate corruption does it drive you to your knees to weep before God and cry out for the nation? Does it stir or prick your heart and cause righteous indignation? Have you become so desensitized that it no longer phases you?

The Bible says the kingdom of God suffers violence, but the violent take it by force. This is a metaphor for intense intercessory prayer. There are many in our communities that have time to commit to praying for our communities, our nation, and global society. Turn off the television, stop watching soap operas, get in the trenches and sharpen your spiritual weapons. The devil is taking no prisoners, he is destroying the souls of our children, families, friends and devastating our nation. When was the last time you took to the street to march for a cause you believed in? When was the last time you wrote a letter to your Representative or Senator regarding a community impacting issue? When was the last time you organized a phone bank to flood Washington, D.C. with calls of support or outrage on legislation? When was the last time you boycotted a business that positioned itself against biblical principles or standards? What are you doing to effect change? It is very sad that we underestimate our ability and think that our voice doesn't count. In understanding the nature of politics we recognize that one plus one plus one plus one equals power. Politics is affected by numbers and money. You are one of the numbers and the money over which you are a steward commands respect. Put your beliefs into action, practice what you preach.

———————●———————

A CALL TO ACTION:

1. Create a network within your church, neighborhood and or community for the purpose of political action; distribute contact information for local, state, and national governing bodies.

2. Designate several people to be gate keepers to watch city council, school board, state and national legislation, court activities; connect with politically active Christian organizations.

3. Get the facts, discuss the issues/candidates from a biblical perspective.

4.   Take action:

a. Local meetings: attend as a group, the more people the louder your voice; select a few articulate speakers; write out your opposition or support statement before hand; know and follow the protocol of the meeting (let all things be done decently and in order) and make your voices heard.

b. Online Support - get a "call to action" email database and participate online with support or opposition e-mails.

c. Write letters; make phone calls, send faxes.

5.   DON'T QUIT OR GIVE UP, if you lose a battle just remember it is not the war. You must continue, there are many rounds in a match. Those that oppose you will never give up. This is a war of attrition and we cannot allow the devil to "wear out the saints." Be diligent, be sober, gird up the loins of your mind and fight the good fight of faith!

You can make a difference, you can effect change. God expects you to walk in the believer's authority with holy boldness and confidence.

CONSIDER POLITICAL OFFICE

We need men and women of faith to run for political office. Look at your local school board, city council, are there any vacancies? Work on someone else's campaign to understand how to get a candidate elected. Attend meetings to familiarize yourself with the workings of the political body in which you are interested in. Contact the Department of Elections to find out about the requirements for filing for an open seat. Take a stand and be counted.

ENDNOTES

Chapter 2, IV. Democrat or Republican, Does It Really Matter:

1. 1961 Commission on Civil Rights, Excerpts from the
    1961 Commission in Civil Rights Report, (Washington
    D.C.; U.S. Government Printing Office, 1961)

2. 2004 National Party Platforms

3. Biographical Directory of the United States Congress,
    1774 - Present

4. John Eidmo, Rulings not Etched in Stone, New American,
    Volume 8, August 2005

5. Justice at the Gates, *Democrats & Republicans in Their
    own Words, National Party of Major Civil Rights
    efforts Based on Side-by-Side Comparison of the
    Early Platforms of the two Major Political Parties*,
    Historical footnotes and annotations by David Barton,
    President of Wallbuilders, (Texas, privately printed n.d.)

6. Justice at the Gates, *Democrats & Republicans in Their
    own Words, National party Platforms on Specific
    Biblical Issues*, (Texas, privately printed n.d.)

7. Lerone Bennett, Jr., Before the Mayflower, A History of
    Black America, Fifth Edition (Penguin Books, Johnson
    Publishing Company, Inc. 1982)

8.   Library of Congress: A Century of Lawmaking for a New
        Nation: U.S. Congressional Documents and Debates,
        1774 - 1875

9.   Robert E. DiClerico and Allan S. Hammock, Points of
        View, (Philippines: Addison Wesley Publishing Company,
        Inc., 1980)

10.   Report on Joint Committee on Reconstruction, Washing-
        ton 1866

11.   Thaddeus Stevens Speech 1865

12.   http://www.spartacus.schoolnet.co.uk

Chapter 3, I. Jefferson Letter

1.   David Barton, Separation of Church and State,
        www.wallbuilders.com
2.   Whistleblower, *The Myth of Church-State Separation*,
        Worldnet Daily, Inc., Grants Pass, OR, Volume 12, No.
        11, November 2003

To order or to schedule voter education workshops
contact publisher or

email: godandgovernment@hotmail.com
P.O. Box 5243
Oakland, CA 94605

www.ingramcontent.com/pod-product-compliance
Lightning Source LLC
Chambersburg PA
CBHW061753050726
47598CB00002B/723